WEDDING TOASTS

Harv Boal

ISBN: 1976453690
ISBN-13: 978-1976453694

Table of Contents

WEDDING TOASTS

INTRO

Wedding toasts are wonderful things!

Traditionally, wedding toasts are words of praise and hope for newly-wed couples, family, and friends—from friends, family, and newly-wed couples. Whether made at wedding rehearsals, wedding receptions, or other wedding events, toasts are well-thought-out words offered as praises, predictions, and prayers for the health and happiness of newly joined couples.

These happy toasts are made by raising high a glass, reciting words of wisdom and/or well wishes and drinking to those praised and wished well.

Unfortunately, this time-honored tradition has been lost—or misunderstood and mistreated in many modern wedding events.

Instead of concise celebratory citations, long, rambling, often confusing, personal stories more about the toast maker than the happy couple have replaced traditional toasts. Usually, they are less inspiring, less fun, and less appropriate. Sorry! It's true.

But that time is gone! It's time to recapture the fun and function and tradition of wedding toasts!

Here are some toasts to replace, or at least improve, introduce or conclude, those rambling personal stories.

Some included in this book are traditional. Others are fun. Some are funky. Choose the ones that best suit your people and event as you prepare for toasting.

You paid for this book, so you can do what you want. Feel free to modify the toasts to suit your own wedding event needs. Change words, phrases, gender references, or situations to make them match your situation and its mood.

Each toast in this book is on its own page so that you have space to add names, change words, and personalize the toast.

Feel free to tear pages out and carry them to the reception, rehearsal, etc. in your pocket. That way this book will be usable, and disposable, and you can buy a new one for the next wedding. Yes, that is good for book sales too!

Most importantly, however you use these toasts, always say them with gusto and good cheer and don't forget to always say,

"Here's to ______ (bride) and _______(groom),"

or

"Let's drink to ________,

or

"Raise high your glass to_______,"

and you'll do fine.

Toast on!

Harv Boal

2018

TRADITIONAL

*M*ay your love

be real

and surreal,

mystical

and magical,

sublime

and prime.

And may you

forever feel

the joy

you know today!

May your days be filled with sunlight,
and your nights filled with stars.

May you spend one hundred years
in each other's arms.

May you always love and cherish
what you have today;
and may the joy of your union
never pass away!

Here's to you, _________ and _______,
a wonderful couple!

_________ *and_____*,

Brand new Mr. and Mrs.,
here's some hugs and
here's some kisses
to each of you
who proved anew
that God still works miracles
and love conquers all!

We, your family and your friends,
wish you joy that never ends!

*O*kay, let's see…

_______________and_______________,

May you live a life that's never friendless,
may your love-making nights be long, even endless.

May your hearts and bank accounts always be full,
and in your home, may love always rule!

Here's to a great couple!

*Y*ou made it at last
and what a cast
of supporting players
are here today to
toast your happiness,
__________and__________.

May today, the best day of your lives so far,
be a dim star in the future constellation
of your shining life together,
and may your love blaze brightly forever!

__________and _______, here's to you!

In your long life together,
may your only disagreements
be about which of you has grown more beautiful
with each passing year.

And may each of you always vote for the other!

______________ and ____________,

Love is much harder than lust,
sort of in the way that steel
is stronger than rust.

May you live a life of steel—
and diamonds,
and titanium
and–you get the idea!

Here's to the bride and groom!

*S*aint and sinner
at the same dinner?
Which one's the winner
is what I must ask
given the task
of making this toast
to surely the most
lucky bride and groom
to ever sit in this room.

One of you is good
and going to get better.
The other, we wonder,
how did you get her?

Raise high your glasses to
_______and ________.

*B*lack and white,
Day and night,
Up and down,
Swim and drown,
Love and hate,
Wall and gate,
Crawl and fly,
Low and high,
Laugh and cry,
Wet and dry—

It's a fact;
Opposites attract.

What can I say?

Well, anyway,
Happy Wedding Day
__________ and __________.

______________and____________,

May you always run life's race
Keeping a perfect pace,
Side by side together,
Regardless of the weather
and may God give you Grace,
Today, Tomorrow, and Forever!

*M*ay you have more patience than pains,
Fewer losses than gains,
More days of sun than rains,
And may your beauty and brains
Always grow with love and grace
As you run the good race,
And may your spouse be okay too.
We all love you_______________and ___________.

*L*ift high your glasses,
my lads and lasses,
with love and pride
that this groom and bride—
both a little odd—
were brought together by God
to this feasting place
by God's amazing grace
and perhaps, it's a rumor,
also by God's sense of humor!

Here's to ________and _______!

_____________**and**_____________,
It's sorta scary
when best friends marry,
but in the end
best spouses are good friends;
so you two have a head start,
already joined heart to heart!

_______________and_________,
May your love grow forever!

Here's to you!

Raise high your glasses to _______and________.

_________________**and**_________________,

Here's a list of three marriage rules that most folks forget
to give new couples, but I promise that following them will
make your marriage better.

Ready?
    1) Never eat peanut butter and crackers in bed.
    2) Never clip your toenails in the living room.
    3) Never trust lists or people who say "Never."

Lift high your glasses now to _________and _______.

_______________**and**_______________,

Here's to the Cupid that put you together,
and here's to the nice(stupid) sunny (rainy)
weather.

Here's to the vows you made today,
and to the fact you neither ran away.

Here's to all the years you'll face ahead,
and here's to tonight's warm wedding bed!

May God bless you in life, whatever may come,
and remember, please, don't do anything dumb!

We love you both!

*M*arriage faces the unfaceable
and embraces the unembraceable.

Marriage bears the unbearable
and dares the undareable.

Marriage is caring and daring.
Marriage is keeping and sharing.

Marriage has nothing to prove
and proves it every day.

Here's to you, ________and _________,
May you be married forever!

_________________**and**_____________________,

May your love flow in endless streams,
and may you achieve all your dreams.

May you find sunshine in your love's face,
and may you live together in peace, love,
and grace
Today, Tomorrow, and Forever.

*M*ay your love always be strong.
May your lives be happy and long.
May you always remember this (month) day,
And may you always say with love everything you say.

Here's to you __________and________.

_______________**and**_______________,

May the songbird of happiness
help you feather your nest
with the twigs of love,
and may your home always be
on strong branches when
winds of time and change blow
the tree of your union.

*H*ere's to the perfect couple
that _____________and_______________are today
and to the reality headed their way
when they sober up!

Lift high the cup
to these married fools;
may they live a life where love always rules.

_________________and_____________,

My wonderful friends,
may the joys of today never end
until the joys of tonight begin.

As you eat and drink and party
may you both be hale and hearty,
but may you save some appetite
for the feast coming later tonight!

__________________and________________,

May your roads be straight and never dusty.
May your nights be long and always lusty.

May your years go on forever.
May you run out of beer never.

May you grab life and embrace it,
and together may you face it
until God calls you home!

*G*od made man
from a pile of dirt
and woman from a rib.
I bet that hurt!

But here today
at this wedding table
we discover God's still able
to take the strangest pair
and give them a life to share!

_______________and_______________,
May your life together
always be one of God's joyous miracles!

*H*ere's to you Mister,
and here's to your Mrs.
May you always share love
and hugs and kisses.

May you have more kids
than you can afford;
and may you always be joyous
in serving Our Lord!

May God bless and keep you always!
Here's to _____________ and _____________.

*M*ay your love last forever,
May your joy end never,
May your friends be clever,
and may you live a hundred years
as husband and wife.

Lift high your glasses to
______________and________.

__________and__________,
May you seldom know grief.
May your quarrels be brief.
May you find relief
in your loved one's arms
--forever!

*M*ay your married journey
be a long and happy path.
In times of trouble
may you help each other laugh.

May your careers be trains
on a long steady track,
and may you consistently
have each other's back.

May you always be faithful,
loving and true,
and may you cherish forever
the day you said "I do."

Here's to ___________ and ________!

*M*an and wife,
Love and life,
Joy and strife:
Opposites attract
And make attractive couples—
And so do you!
Here's to you _________ and _________ !

__________and __________,

Here's to you.

Remember that marriage is all about ation.

You know like:

Moderation,

Consternation,

Adoration,

Adaptation,

Cooperation:

May you have them all.

And maybe some

Sensation too!

*R*aise high your glasses
Lads and lasses,
Drink your wedding drink!

Today these two
Sit here before you
And tonight—
Well, what do you think?

Here's to _________ and_______,
May you live and love long!

*H*ere's to _____ and to _______:
May your joys be many
and your problems be few;
may God always guide
and protect both of you.

May you prize your love,
your hopes and your dreams;
and may you flourish
in God's green fields and quiet streams
Today, Tomorrow and Forever!

*H*ere's to you,
you lucky two.
May you find success
in all you do.

May you be faithful and true
through sunshine and
through stormy weather,
and may you love each other forever.

Here's to _________ and _________!

*H*ere's to _________and ___________ .

May your love be a legend
for generations that come after.
May you learn how to turn
tears into laughter.
May you find beauty and grace
in your lover's face,
and may God bless you
and all that you do!

Lift your glasses to _______and_______ .

*M*ay you hold each other tight
through the stormy night
of life, facing strife,
Together.

May you every day
adore each other more
than the day before.

May you sing in spring,
Snuggle in winter,
Stand tall in fall,
and swim naked in
summer's ponds
for a thousand years.

_____and_____, we love you!

*I*n your life together,
May love be your rule,
shunning all that's cruel,
standing side by side
with grace and truth and pride
knowing in the end
your spouse is your best friend.

Here's to ____________and____________.

*H*ere's to _____ and _______,
May you always find shelter
in the arms of each other,
and may your definition
of "home" be wherever
you are together!

And may you be together forever!

*B*efore a fireplace on a rug,
at the day's end sharing a hug
or on the sofa watching tv,
may you be happy together
wherever you may be.

Here's to ____ and _____ and their life
together!

Countryside,
Cityside,
Fireside,
Ringside,
High tide,
Worldwide,
wherever life leads you,
may you be groom and bride
side by side
forever!

Lift your glasses high to _____and______.

_______________and _______________,

Wherever life leads you
may you go now as two
who have become one.

And may your oneness
be wonderful!

*H*ere's to __________and__________,

At the coffee shop
and the traffic stop
and the shopping mall
and the market stall,
at home in bed
and inside your head,
may you find
a home together
forever!

*M*ay you gain stature,
but not weight.
May you grow wise
without learning hate.
May you overcome fears,
cry only happy tears,
and enjoy a thousand years
as husband and wife.
In others words..
May you have a perfect life!

Here's to ____and_____!

________________and________________,

I wish for you, the perfect couple,
a house with a yard and a fence,
silly humor and common sense,
family and friends,
and love that never ends.

  We lift our glasses high to You!

*W*hat makes a good marriage?

Comfortable shoes,
church pews,
jazz and the blues,
limited world news.

What makes a good marriage?

Walks in the park,
embraces in the dark,
a daily loving remark,
making home a safe ark.

What makes a good marriage?

You do,
you two.
here's to you!

*H*ere's to ____ and _____,

May you camp by pure water
and swim in silver streams.
May you work in daylight
and dance in moonbeams.
May you cherish all your days
and find the night's delights.
May you live a thousand years,
always striving for new heights!

*H*ere's to the new hubby
and to the new wife:
May you live long
and have a happy life.

May you be joyful
in all you do,
and may God bless
and keep you
Together
Forever!

*M*ay your love double
in times of trouble,
and may sorrows flee
way rapidly
in the face
of your love and grace.

Your love inspires us all!

Here's to _____ and_____!

*M*ay today, your wedding day,
be the beginning of
a new way of life
filled with joy and love,
and may every day
after today
witness your growth
in unity and union.

Here's to you _______ and_______ !

*M*ay the road of your life
be free from stress and strife,
and may every exit and side street
that you follow be sweet;
and may your journey
Begin,
Continue,
And End
In love!

Here's to _____and_____!

*A*in't it great
to celebrate,
to share a plate
and a bottle
with these new mates?

Ain't it grand
to understand
how a woman and a man
are united today
by God's plan?

Here's to you_____and_____!

*T*oday,
one plus one
equals one.
All the old
two stuff is done.

There's so much work
and so much fun
to being married,
but don't be worried.

You two—no you one—were meant for each other!

A whole life planned
to be hand in hand--
ain't it grand?

A hundred years
of laughter and tears
hopes and fears.

An eternity
to learn to be
in harmony.

These are my hopes for
you _____ and _____.

*M*ay all your kisses be long and sweet;
May warm socks protect you from cold feet;
May your love grow stronger every day,
and may God guide you in all your ways
as you travel your lifelong path
with a song, a tear, and a laugh
Forever and a Day.

*I*t all begins today
in a wonderful way
called a wedding,
and we're all betting
it will last forever
as they grow together
in love and in joy,
a girl and a boy
becoming woman and man
according to God's plan.

May you find your destiny
as, united, you learn to be
our Creator's greatest creation—
A Happily Married Couple.
Here's to you ____and ____!

"*E*ver after! Ever after!
Years of joy and laughter,"
that's what we all say
we wish for you today,
but really there's more;
we want you to soar
held up by angels' wings
to great and greater things,
as your years accumulate,
to build a marriage that's great
and loving and grand,
just as the Creator planned
when He brought you together!

Here's to _____ and_____!

*R*ing the bells
everywhere.
Make some noise;
we don't care!

Now's the time
to celebrate!
Here's the new couple;
ain't they great?

You're the best, _____and_____.
Here's to You!

*M*ay our good God
give to you
many long years
traveling through
His wide creation,
and may your shared love
be like His from above—
eternal and perfect.

Here's to ____ and _____,
Now and forever!

Cry, "Nonny, nonny, hey!"
on this wedding day
for a couple of wonderful friends!

Lift your glasses high
beneath a perfect sky
for a love that never ends.

Cry, "Hey, nonny, nonny!"
for a bride so bonnie
and her handsome groom.

Lift high your glasses,
my lads and lasses,
to the newest couple in the room!

*M*ay your joys be many
and your sorrows be few.

May you never lack a penny,
but still prosper if you do.

May you walk every mile,
unless you can ride,
facing life with a smile,
with laughter and pride.

Mays the vows you made
on this wedding day
be your sun and your shade
as you live, work, and play.

And may God bless and keep you
forever together!

Here's to you ______and_____!

*D*rink to this woman,
drink to this man,
drink to the life
they've got planned.

Drink to the husband
and drink to the wife;
wish them both
a happy married life.

Drink to the vows
we all heard them say,
and pray that they keep them
forever and a day!

Raise your glasses high to _____and_____!

*E*very girl and guy,
lift your glasses high.
Let the world
hear us cry,
"Huzzah to man and wife,"
Hurrah for married life!
Goodbye to singles' strife!
Huzzah, hurrah, hooray;
God bless your wedding day!"

Here's to you,
_____and _____,
one made from two.
Huzzuh, hurrah, hooray!
God bless your wedding day!

*A*s your marriage
is about to start,
may God hold you
in the palm of his hand
and keep you close to His heart.

And may you find
peace, love, and joy
in all you do
as Our Lord makes
a miraculous one
from a wonderful two!

Here's to _____ and _____!

*M*ay love be your parasol
when life shines too hot,
your umbrella when pain rains,
and your life boat
when disaster threatens;
and may you lovingly
weather together
the cold nights and hot days
of destiny's deserts,
cherishing the gift of each other
until God calls you home
to Paradise.

Here's to _____ and _____,
a match made in Heaven!

*T*o ______ and _____,
may you face
your married race
with joy and grace,
having fun
as you run
down the course
for better or worse,
in sickness and health,
through poverty and wealth,
and may your run,
when it's done,
be recalled as one
honoring God's Son
who runs today
and all the way
with you!

*H*ey, husband and wife,
may your new life
progress without strife,
and may your years
have more joy than tears
as you face together
all life's weather;
and may you share love and laughter
now and forever after!

Here's to you _____ and ____!

*H*ere's a toast
to our hosts
here today.
Cry "Hooray"
and raise a glass
to a lovely lass
and handsome groom
filling this room
with their joy,
a girl and a boy
becoming woman and man
according to God's plan!

Bless you both, _____ and _____!
Here's to you!

_____ and _____,
at this marriage start,
you are close to God's heart.
May you follow His perfect plan
and live in the shelter of His hand
in three-part harmony,
now and eternally!

*M*ay smooth roads rise up to meet you.
May life's trials never defeat you.
May you have the courage to face
every step of your race
with dignity and pride,
and may your love abide
now and always
for all of your days.

Here's to you _____ and _____!

FUNKY

*T*ake a break
from your steak
and wedding cake.

Here's your chance
to pose and prance,
sing and dance.

Now's the time
for song and rhyme,
to have a good time.

Here's to you,
You lucky two,
And your union too!

Live long and love longer!

*B*ride and groom,
Get a room!
You and your kisses.

Do you think that we
really like to see
you acting like Mr. and Mrs.?

You bet we do!

________________and________________,

We lift our glasses to you,
because the table weighs too much
and has shiny decorations we might break;
but there is no obstacle you can't overcome
if you keep loving each other as you do today.

But, still, raise your glasses, not the table, to
_____and______ because raising the table
might upset candles and start a fire and the
family would lose their deposit on this room
and they're already angry with me for
introducing _________and ________ and I
guess I'll just sit down now… but here's to
you!

*H*ere's to the bride and to the groom,
the best-looking folks in the room.

Here's to the parents who footed the bill
and to all their friends drinking their fill.

Here's to a joyful wedding day
and to a wedding night of---well, anyway,

Here's to _____and _____and to you all!

Congrats _____________and_____________.

*W*ith vows and "Wows!"
you're married now.
Just be cool.
Don't have a cow.
Hold each other tight
day and night.
Marriage is about love,
not about fright.
Alright?
Alright!

Here's to ___and____,
two cool folks
becoming a married miracle!

*G*room and bride
unified;
what a ride!
Now your love
is magnified!

Two become one?
Sounds like fun!
Get it done!

Here's to _____and ______,
the real deal.

To _________and_________,

May your bed be soft when life is hard!

*T*he food is great,
The drink is good.
Everything surely should
last forever--knock on wood—
and celebrate!

Here's to ______and_______!

*L*ook at them all aglow.
Must be love, don't you know?
May they shine and never rust.
May they always—oops, it's lust!

*T*his couple has everything:
They have elegance,
old sweat pants,
a rusty car,
a favorite bar,
family and friends,
and love without ends.

Here's to _____and______!

________and________,

Here's some marriage advice I collected
from some of your elders. You might want
to take notes.

To be happy in marriage do the following
things:

Always love and share.
Buy a comfortable chair.
Wear clean underwear,
or none at all.

Trust each other.
Listen to your mother.
Cherish sister and brother,
but make your own decisions.

Dress for the weather.
Have adventures together.
Buy shoes made of leather,
but not bras or briefs.

Good grief!

Here's to you _____ and _____!

__________and ___________,
Sitting beneath a tree,
k.i.s.s.---wait a minute,
you're married?
Get a room!
Get a life!
Get going!
Get….well, you get it.
We love you, you big nuts!

Raise high your glasses to _______and_________!

*R*oses are red
and violets are blue.
There's a big bed
calling you two.
So eat and drink
but not too much.
I don't really think
you want to be out of touch
tonight?
Am I right?

*Y*ou can't hide,
you groom and bride.
We know you
want to do
the hootchy koo
all night through.

But we have fears
you'll strip your gears
and collapse in tears
if you have any more beers.

So slow down the pace, just a bit.
It's not a race; try to enjoy it.
Today is your only wedding
but you'll have years for bedding.

*T*he beer is warm.
The fish is cold.
Bridemaids and groomsmen
are getting alcohol bold.

The great music and open bar
have pushed your rating up to "R."
It's time take the children home
before libidos start to roam
and parents filled up with champagne
wake up with too much to explain.

So, bride and groom,
clear the room.
Send all these fuzzied heads
home to their married beds.

And maybe you can find one too?
Wahoo!

*O*kay, you two.
We get it. You're married.
We lost the bet.
Someone was crazy enough to marry ______.
Somebody was lucky enough to marry __________.
Bookies around the world are amazed.
Many of us here lost a fortune.
I hope you're happy.

Something borrowed,
something green,
something tonight
almost obscene:
I love the old wedding sayings.

Married in the rain,
a lifetime of pain;
married in the sun,
too cheap to rent the chapel.
you know that one?

Early to kiss,
and early to wed,
makes a couple
socially dead?
Another favorite.

Don't disparage
love and marriage?
Not bad either.

But this one, this one's for you two.
Don't fight
at night
under the covers;
be lovers
and morning
without warning
will be better.

*D*rinking champagne
and throwing rice,
we can't complain,
are sort of nice,
but in this room
the bride and groom,
aren't nice
or cool
or plastic—
they're fantastic!

Here's to _________and_____________!

*M*ay the horned toad of happiness
hop your way
every day.

May the ants in your pants
making you dance
be a mutual itch.

May you grow old together
but live forever
in the lives you touch.

*M*ay every wedding you attend after today,
no matter how grand or fun,
make you just a little bit sad
because none of them measure up to today.

*U*p and down,
sage and clown,
light and dark,
meow and bark,
opposites attract;
that's a fact.
And so I say
here today
let's cry hooray
for man and wife,
short years but long life
free from strife.
So hugs and kisses
for the new Mr. and Mrs.
Here's to you,
You Fabulous Two!

*M*ay your marriage
age like fine wine,
and may you always
have cheese and crackers!

Here's to you _____ and _____!

*M*ay your awesome love,
like a woolen glove,
be warm and fitting.

May your laughter and joy,
like a kid's new toy,
be exciting.

And may your future be
secure and bright,
like coming daylight.

May you shine on!

*M*y wish for you,
you newlywed two,
is beaches sandy,
calorie-free candy,
warm winters,
painless splinters,
days of sun
and nights of fun,
good friends and peers
for all your years!

Here's to you, _____ and _____!

*A*in't it grand
how God planned
in His grace
for the human race
to use His might
to bless and unite
you two today
in this wonderful way?
I say, "Hooray!"

Here's to _____ and _____!

*H*ere's wishing _____ and _____
warm shoes
and cold brews,
lots of money,
tea with honey.
moonlit nights,
short-lived fights,
happy tears
and a hundred years
getting better
together
forever!

*W*e're all crazy,
the human race;
your friends threw birdseed
at your face today
and cried, "Hooray,
you're married."
Did you feel harried
or upset?
No. So, I bet,
you will survive
and even thrive
in the years ahead.

Live long and prosper, _______ and _______!

A pledge and a vow,
and presto and wow,
you're husband and wife
with a brand new life;
imagine that,
like a rabbit from a hat
or a coin choosing to appear
from behind your ear,
your love is magical,
wonderful, amazing,
and blazing!

May it always be so;
we love you, you know!

Here's to _____ and _____!

*B*eneath the lace,
behind the tie,
there's a girl
and there's a guy
for removed from fancy scenes,
a couple wearing faded blue jeans.

After the cake
and the honeymoon,
there's a bride
and there's a groom
napping together
on a Sunday afternoon.

Down through the years
despite laughter and tears
through good and bad weather,
they face life together,
partners in all they do—
that's my wish for you!

Here's to you ______and_____!

A cold drink,
a warm bed,
blushes pink,
a level head,
robust loins,
happy tears,
golden coins,
and a hundred years—
these are my wishes for you,
you marvelous two!

Here's to ______ and ______!

*H*ere's to union
and to communion,
to endless caring
and eternal sharing.

Here's wishing you two,
in everything you do,
blessings without endings
in receivings and sendings.

May your marriage be
a song of grace and harmony,
and may God, loving and grand,
make your duet a band
making beautiful music together.

Raise your glasses and your voices
to _____and _____!

Hurray for them!

*L*et's shout "Hooray"
for this wedding day
and lift our voices
'cuz they made good choices,
after years of dates,
in choosing their mates;
and now they're together
and it couldn't be better.
So lift your glasses high
and shout to the sky
"Here's to ______and_______!

You crazy two!
What did you do?
When others said,
"Marriage is dead,"
you didn't care.
You said, "We dare!"

You believed in love
and believed in vows.
You stood above
the heres and nows.

You did it today
the old-fashioned way,
and here you stand
wife and husband.

Here's to you,
the throwback two!

*G*orgeous dresses,
hair-sprayed tresses,
polished shoe toes,
spiffy tuxedoes;
you all look great
so I hesitate
to ask for more,
but today I implore
God to bless you two
in all you do,
today and tonight
and even next week,
as you happily seek
to build a life
Together!
Forever!

*H*ere's to you,
you lovely two,
looking so cute
in dress and suit
as we all see
it was meant to be;
the perfect pair
sitting right there
side by side
groom and bride,
husband and wife
ready for life,
together—forever!

Here's to _____and_____!

Here's to the best union
since sugar and spice,
a couple just as easily nice
as peanut butter and jelly,
just as cool as Regis and Kelly,
just as stylish as black and white,
as complementary as day and night,
better than sweet potatoes and ham,
meant to be together like email and spam,
stronger than steel and rust,
bonded like country roads and dust,
the perfect couple in every way:
what else can anyone say
except, congratulations to you,
you star-eyed two!
We lift our glasses to _____ and _____!

Specialized

The beauty and the nerd

I once heard
that a beauty
and a nerd
did not compute,
but I'm here
to dispute,
cuz the point
is moot.
They're so damn cute!

Raise your glasses high to ____and _____!

For the investors/bankers

____________________and__________________,

May your love today
like a 401 (K)
grow stronger the longer
you invest and pray;

And may you discover
in a hundred years
that grace and love always pay
the best dividends
and that true love never ends.

The fairytale couple

Once upon a time,
this afternoon,
a princess bride
and a studly groom
dined together in a feasting room.

She was beautiful
and he was grand
as they ate and drank
with their friends
just as planned.

They're still here now
sharing love and laughter,
and I'm here to say
"Have a happy ever after!

Here's to _________and ______, a royally cool couple!

The other fairytale couple

Perhaps fairy tales do come true.
Just look at the two of you,
Beauty and the Beast
at a wedding feast,
sitting side by side,
wedded groom and bride.

Today some people cried
and children ran to hide
but they say love is blind
so perhaps today we find
it's all really true,
so here's to you.

May your love be long and strong
and the stuff of movies and song.

Raise your glasses to a fairytale couple,
___________and_______________.

The fantasy fans

May your destiny
be a story of mystery,
chivalry and harmony
eternally!

May you live in a castle
far from the hassle
of business dragons
and family thrones.

May you fight side by side
with valor and pride
but find a warm place to hide
when winter comes.

_____and_____, here's to you!

Other fantasy fans

May no trolls rise up to meet you
and no dragons to defeat you
as you storm the castle walls
and swim in waterfalls.

And may you live with love and laughter,
Today and forever after!

_______________and _____________,
You are a couple that inspires legends!

For the "not so young" couple

Here's to ____________ and ____________,
not the youngest couple to ever wed.

She doesn't see he's going bald.
He always comes when he's called.

She know he snores but doesn't care;
he never mentions her graying hair.

They're still young in their hearts,
although we all know they're really old f---ts.

My dear friends,
may you be forever young!

For scientists

Science says energy and matter
are interchangeable,
but it doesn't matter
how energetic your marriage is
if you don't have love—
but ____________and ______you two do—
so never change.

Here's to ______and ______.

From Grandma

I am here, my dear,
To tell you with candor
A grandson is like a son
Only grander.

Take care of my boy,
Live your lives with joy,
And I'll be happy for you
And, please, call me "Grandmother" too.

Lift your glasses to _________and________.

Grandparent to grandson

Here's to my grandson and his lovely wife:
May you find happiness together all your life.

May your love be strong as you walk together along
the roads of marriage, parenthood, careers and family.

And may you stand together one day to toast
the marriages of your grandchildren.

Friends and family,
Lift high your glasses to ______________and________.

Father of the bride to son-in-law

________________, my new son-in-law, today I gave you my daughter's hand. But _______years ago when she was born, I gave __________my heart. So today you've accepted a lot of responsibility.

I pray God gives you the courage and strength to handle it well. If you don't, I'm too old and too wise to even pretend I could protect you from her mother.

Here's to the new couple! May they love and cherish each other forever!

From father of groom

Here's to my son__________and his wife____________.

________________, son, you were born male and grew up as
a boy, but today you become a man, a husband, and a
partner.

Only men can be husbands. Boys and males fail.

Be a man for _______________, son. Love her. Cherish her.
Embrace her.

And _________, today we are proud you are the woman we
welcome to our family.

Here's to__________and __________, man and woman!

Groom's mom to new daughter-in-law

A mother bears a son and raises him
to love and respect women. And then
she gives him away to another woman,
praying her new "daughter" has learned
the same lessons, and that she will love
and respect her son.

You,__________, are the wife that I would
choose for_____________ so I am so happy
you have chosen each other.

May you love and respect each other
 all the days of your lives.

Here's to __________and_____________.

From the bride's brother

Here's to the mister that just married my sister.
You have my best wishes for today and tomorrow,
And my promise to help in times of joy and sorrow.

I'm your man whenever you need me,
but if I show up you better promise to feed me!

Here's to ____________and ________________.

Bride's sister to the couple

They say a man chases and chases a woman—
until she catches him!

I say "Lucky catch" to both of you.
We're all so glad you both said "I do."

Here's to you my sister,
and to you my new brother;
I thank God you found each other.

Groom's father to couple

Here's to my favorite only son
and to the woman crazy enough to marry him.
May you two find in your union the joy your mother and I
have shared for ___________years.

May you face life's challenges and adventures hand in
hand; and may you discover soon that I am currently the
perfect age to be a grandfather.

Lift high your glasses to ___________and___________.

From the bride's brother

Here's to a man I call "brother,"
born technically to another mother,
but my best friend all of my life.

And here's to his beautiful wife,
a woman I'm proud to call my sister.
He'd have been a chump if he had missed her!

Here's to you _________ and______________.

Best man to groom

Yep, okay, you're the groom,
but the real best man in the room,
is lifting his glass here today
to tell the world you're okay
in your own crazy way.

Kind and sane through and through
until you've had a beer or two.
Fearless and bold
with a level head
until you catch a cold
and hide in bed.

Always kind,
never out of sorts
till you lose your mind
watching sports.

So you're no saint,
what can I say?
You still married an angel today.

Here's to you ______and______!

For Couples With Children

Here's to you and to you and to your children too.

To ________and________and______, etc.

May your new union be not only a union of two people but
a union of your families, you and your children,
a union of hearts and minds, of spirits and lives,
that will make all of you—and the world—a better place
because you are living and sharing life
as family and as friends.
Here's to all of you.

From the pastor—

May peace and joy
come to you,
you blessed two,
and may all you do
be done in fun
and in love,
and may God above
hold you in his hands
and make wonderful plans
for this he and she
for eternity.

Here's to ______and______!

From the groom's best friend to the couple—

Such a lovely dame—
Ain't it a shame
she chose this guy?
I don't know why.
Such a lucky jerk,
Be sure you always work
to be the best you can
for this great wo—man.

And you, brand new missus,
give him hugs and kisses;
beneath his ho hum hide
he had the brains inside
to pick you for his bride.

So love on and live
and celebrate;
you both picked the perfect mate!

Here's to _____and______!

From an old family friend—

Here's to the bride and to the groom,
the loveliest couple in the room,
and here's to their long married life,
may it be full of joy and free of strife.

May you face all seasons and weather,
through the strength of being together,
and may you be happy, loyal, and free
from now until eternity.

Here's to _____and_____!

For travelers—

May life's long miles
widen your smiles
as you journey along
with laughter and song;
and may the obstacles you face
take a distant second place
to your love and devotion.

Here's to the road traveled well
and traveled together!

Raise your glasses to _____and ______!

From the new couple to all their parents—

Here's to the greatest parents in the house,
the ones who raised us each a wonderful spouse.

Thank-you, Dad(s) and Mom(s),
for all the hard work you've done.

You made a person perfect for me
through years of sweat, tears, and tenacity.

We both hope we can someday too
be role models just like you.

Here's to ___and ____!

For the "Greens"---

May you hike every path
with a map and a laugh;
may you drink from crystal streams.

May you lay down your heads
on pine-scented beds
and only have fair-forest dreams.

May your coffee be fair trade
and your whole life hand made,
avoiding tired clichéd schemes.

May you keep growing stronger
as your journey grows longer
and discover what love really means!

Here's to _____ and _____!

Hike on!

From an aunt or uncle---

May your years be many.
May you never lack a penny.
May your days be filled with sun.

May your health be great,
and may you always debate
which of you is the luckiest one.

You both chose well;
we know you're swell,
so here's my wish for you—

May you have wedded bliss
and anniversaries of this
for a hundred years, plus two!

Here's to _____ and _____!

From grandparent(s) to the new couple---

_____ and _____,
may you live happily ever after,
sharing a long happy life
as husband and wife;
and may your love and laughter
be an inspiration
for many a generation
that follows you, you wonderful two!

I love you!
Here's to you!

TOAST ON!

Harv Boal's books unite traditions of the past with hopes of today and dreams for tomorrow.

Check out his works at Amazon.

Fiction
Peace of Kake
Berth Day Kake
Vetting Kake
Original Thin

Poetry
Dead Grandma Knows
Ain't No Saint
Down at Café Ole
Daily Demotions

NonFiction
A Wee Bit Wicked: The Unintentional Evil of Small Churches

All books are available at Amazon.com
Follow Harv at harvboal.wordpress.com